Two Heavy Words

Two Heavy Words

Reflections of a First-Year Missionary

M. J. Weissenberger

RESOURCE *Publications* · Eugene, Oregon

TWO HEAVY WORDS
Reflections of a First-Year Missionary

Resource Publications
An Imprint of Wipf and Stock Publishers
199 W. 8th Ave., Suite 3
Eugene, OR 97401

www.wipfandstock.com

ISBN 13: 978-1-62564-433-6

Manufactured in the U.S.A.

Contents

Preface

I DO NOT MEAN, in writing this book, to presume any assumptions that no book on this subject has ever been written. I am simply a writer with a story to tell and a Christian journey to share.

When I graduated college and entered the mission field in Bolivia I found that many assumptions I had made about missions and my own theological framework were ignorantly misinformed. My transition was not as easy as it could have been and my struggles were the result of years without proper spiritual disciplines. I feel now as if my ignorance stood in the way of my own survival.

I wrote on a blog almost daily in an attempt to process everything that was happening to me. I was trying to stay connected with the friends and family I had back in the United States, and my blog was sort of an intermediate home between North and South America. Now that I can stare back at those entries, at a separate time in my life, I can see the great divides in my heart that prevented me from willingly obeying all of the Lord's commands in my life.

To say that the mission field is a place of struggle is to state the obvious. It is not, in its nature, intended to be a war for the missionary. I had thought before going to Bolivia that the only "war" I would encounter would be opposition to the word of God. I did not realize that the greater war would be within my own heart fighting a culture that had subdued my passion for Christ.

This book is not a chastisement of the American church or the American Christian culture. It is not meant to be a guide for every missionary preparing to go overseas. It is simply a reflection on the transition of one college student to the mission field. It is a series of revelations that the Lord placed upon my heart to change my soul forever. My journey was full of adventure, excitement, despair, and regret. We have much to learn from our successes and our failures, and it is my hope that these stories teach you as much as they have taught me.

1

Ball and chain

THERE COMES A POINT in any person's life when they realize the gravity of words. Perhaps it is a motivational speaker who must choose carefully his immortalized phrases, a mother in recoil of her harsh tone toward her children, or even a politician whose racial slur is now plastered on the front page of every news source. No matter the circumstances, the realization that your words have meaning beyond a singular moment can cause the greatest of fears.

I can remember sitting in my dorm in the spring of my senior year of college with my heart racing. My eyelids brimmed with tears and I was ready to give up on life only because the words that I had promised were actually coming true. The words I didn't even know I had meant to say were being called upon and my very nature was being questioned. Did I really mean it?

I had made the severe mistake of telling the Lord two words. And by "severe mistake" I do not imply that they were in any way regrettable; I simply attempt to draw attention to the singular fact that for once in my life I was being forced to put my money where my mouth was.

I had been searching for affection and value my entire life and to no avail. I attempted outlandish schemes to gain jealousy and compliments from my peers and family members as a teenager. I had volunteered and performed past my physical capacity and I toiled endlessly for the sake of feeling righteous and admired. When it all came down to it, my senior year of college, I was faced with the question: "What next?"

I did what I thought was logical and began to apply for graduate school. After all, they say no good jobs want only a bachelor's degree these days. I was half honest with myself in believing that I wanted to go to grad school in order to secure a good job and peruse the greater depths of my field. The other half that I ignored was that somewhere inside of me I had become convinced of the idea that I would make my family proud and would be more respected if I earned an even higher degree.

It was at the rejection of this notion when the Lord helped shake me into the reality that he had no intention of me attending graduate school. In fact, he was calling me to something far different. He continually showed me passage upon passage in scripture of people who left their home at his call—Abraham, Moses, Jonah, Jesus, the Twelve Apostles. He was repeatedly showing me the needs on this planet and how my only goal in graduate studies was to glorify myself. My entire life had led up to me becoming a missionary even though the sinews of my soul were holding strong to an old blanket of security.

So one night while praying before falling asleep, I half-heartedly whispered the words: "I'll go."

If I had known how the Lord would hold me accountable to that promise? I might not have said them at the time. I had just started a relationship with a man two years younger than me, I was beginning an internship for student teaching while trying to figure out how to survive it, and I was planning my own life as if the Lord was not remotely involved in it.

Earlier that evening I had been humming an old song we used to sing at my church as a child. The last line especially repeated in my head. Out of sheer curiosity, I searched an online concordance for those lyrics to see if they came from scripture. After being rerouted to Psalm 51, I discovered that the original words were: "Restore to me the joy of thy salvation and uphold me with a willing spirit" (Ps 51:12 RSV).

This was hardly alarming news to me at the time, but it was interesting enough that I mulled over it while preparing for bed. By the time I began to set my alarms on my clock for the early morning, I was considering what my life would look like if my spirit was willing. And what exactly did I need to be willing to do? To go to a foreign land? To leave my home like Abraham and wander as a nomad for the sake of God's people? I was imagining living in a rice patty somewhere, my knees deep in the water and wearing a conical hat. I laughed away the image.

So as I climbed into bed, weary and downtrodden from another day not focused on the Lord or his plan for my life, I almost jokingly said "I'll go."

Four months later I found myself raising funds so that I could serve as a missionary teacher for a year of my life in South America. The moment those two lead-weight words left my lips, it was if the ball and chain were bound to my feet. I was headed on a way road to Bolivia, no matter the opposition.

2

Learning his love

RAISING SUPPORT IS HARD. It's not physical work that tires your muscles or breaks a sweat—but it certainly can tear your heart into pieces, especially if your heart does not understand God's.

So I had said my two words and put myself on a one-way fast track to teach in Bolivia. I didn't really know what to do next. It was March and I still had ten weeks left in my student teaching, graduation, and moving out to accomplish. Support raising was put on the back burner and lumped with the notion that if this was God's desire for me, he would provide my way. Besides, I thought flippantly, doesn't it say somewhere in the book Matthew that if God cares for the sparrows how much more will he care for me?

A wonderful lady from my mission had me starting the process of creating a support letter. If you have never set out to write a support letter before, welcome to one of the most frustrating processes of your life. I'm a writer by nature and getting my thoughts on paper is extremely easy, but, asking others for money and getting them excited about a mission is not the same as explicating a passage of

Shakespeare. A college essay displays intelligence; a support letter displays humility.

Though the lady from my mission had emailed and called multiple times, I simply wasn't motivated. To be honest, I was staring in the face of my $22,000 goal wondering how it would ever come true. I was trying to figure out what magical combination of words would coax the average American to pour their hard-earned cash into my support account despite the economic recession and the fact that I had a teaching degree and could be paid by a school district to do this job in America. I made multiple drafts, all of which sounded like glorified cow dung, and finally settled on something a little less than cliché, but definitely filled with pictures of me and children from previous mission trips for dramatic effect.

In April, that same wonderful woman from my mission called me on the phone asking about follow-up phone calls, as if I'd actually called anyone like she'd told me to. I have no idea what kind of an excuse I gave her, but I know it did not make her happy. Let's be honest—I was knee deep in executing my unit plan on *The Adventures of Huckleberry Finn* across five sections of eleventh grade English as a student teacher. I was not about to just use up my free time to call people and ask if they had received my letter and were considering donating to my mission. I looked around at myself and could only think: "What free time?"

So life went on. May came, I graduated, and my best friend and I hopped on a plane down to her aunt's house in Florida to spend a glorious week relaxing on the beach and being as lazy as we wanted, evading all possible responsibility in our lives. It was any girl's dream.

Until I flew home to realize it was June, I was supposed to be on a plane in July, and I had received $150 of my $22,000.

At this point I was ignoring the calls from my mission in a full panic. There was absolutely no way this was happening. It was beyond all reasoning and beyond all hope. Even if every person I knew gave me money, these things take time. I was just one person and it was all out of my hands.

That's when I started to pray. Four months after I had been appointed by my mission, I finally chose to pray about my circumstances. I was in a state of distress and knew that only God could provide these funds in such a short period of time. I also was unwilling to accept the responsibility of my laziness. So the praying and the crying cycle began, occasionally accompanied by ice cream. But still, there was no new money in my ministry account.

I was online one afternoon in mid-June when my husband's father started up a chat conversation. My husband and I were dating at the time, but his father and I had grown close and I always appreciated his advice. He was a comforter, always waiting for the moment to fix. So while I droned on and on about my woes and the trials of support raising, he finally said: "The personal challenge that most of us face is the truth that some things are able to be changed, but that we are not willing to make the sacrifice necessary to do so. It becomes a reflection of the true value that we place on things. Most people would rather live in denial or make excuses. So, is the task impossible or merely difficult?"

I was incapable of replying. My cursor blinked in the text box over and over again until I minimized the entire page trying to calculate how much value this missionary experience had for me at that moment. Once assessed as having indefinite worth, with tears in my eyes, I told him that my task was difficult, not impossible, and he asked how I felt.

"Like a sitting duck," I typed. "I am frustrated because I have attempted to tackle problems and have seen no results, so now I'm seeking the counsel of others."

"That is a mature response to the recognition that your initial approach failed," he replied. "Frustration is emotion. The difference between frustration and self-pity is the direction your thoughts are facing—inwardly or outwardly. So, my advice to the duck would be to move."

I wanted to laugh. I really did. But all I could think, and type, was: "Move where?!"

And then it occurred to me that I had never asked God what to actually do about it all. I had simply come to him, blaming him for my circumstance, and begging for money. I never asked how to accomplish what he had set before me. After being picked up and dusted off, I returned in prayer and was finally given the courage to follow-up with phone calls on the letters I'd sent out. I was given some hope. And on top of it all, I decided to pray small, because I assumed small prayers get answered. I prayed for at least $500 that day. God gave me $3200.

As to be expected, I cried tears of joy. But then I sat on it. I thought the next day would be just as profitable, and it wasn't. I made no phone calls. I wrote no letters. I simply expected the funds to start rolling in now that I'd done something. Ten days later I was still 65 percent away from full financial support and trying to figure out how to make God bring the money in faster, which was the true root of my problems.

I was talking with my husband's father another day and we got on to the topic of his family and how much he loves them. At one point he asked me about the love in my family. I thought about it intently and realized I'd had the notion for years that I felt like I had to deserve love. I felt the need to perform in order to become loved.

I broke down crying when it dawned upon me that I was using this support raising process as a means of trying to feel loved by God. On the day I received $3200, I had prayed for only $500 because I did not truly believe God loved me. I felt like a nuisance even asking God for money, let alone people I knew. I wasn't just letting him love me or care for me—I was forcing him to show me love in specific ways because I needed to see his love in order to have faith and believe that it was real.

But what a hypocrite was I? Anytime someone had requested a gift for their birthday and then made it very clear that they would be extremely disappointed if they did not get *that* exact gift, I didn't really want to get it for them. I felt like my hands were tied and I was not able to show them love; I was only able to get in a car and run them an errand. Does not the same principal apply to God? Is the fact that he does not necessarily do what I ask him to do a true measurement of the depths of his love? Would not his love be more evident through the giving of gifts that I need just because he knows I need them? Additionally, how much greater are his gifts since he is immutable and knows what I need to prepare me for my future that he has planned?

So I went back to the praying and crying cycle to come to the point of confession on my pathetically sad view of God. I was shocked into the reality that God's love is not monetary and that I could do nothing to increase his love, decrease his love, or quantify it. Two days later, my total financial support increased by 20 percent. I will add that these increases were continually slow because if I had received all of my remaining balance in one day, I would not have spent enough time reflecting on the nature of his love and rooting up my own false theology.

God would not give me what I needed until I could understand why he gives. Though it would take much more than these few months to teach me about the reality of the relationship a Christian has with God, it was the beginning of the editing process of my soul. Having grown up attending church and spending my college years in a student ministry, I had assumed my theology was soundly developed. It did not yet occur to me that my culture had been at war with my theology for the entirety of my life.

I can remember sitting through many sermons growing up that focused on what I ought to do throughout the journey of my faith, or how I ought to act or conduct myself. I can remember sermons on what other people have done and what the men and women documented in the scriptures have done. I cannot easily remember many compelling sermons on how God's character is immutable so that what he has done is what he is doing and what he will continue to do, and how all of that is deeply rooted in his love.

I do not contend that this lack of understanding was a result of the churches I attended. It very well could have been my personal refusal to listen. Either way, the result stands that as a twenty-two year-old college graduate, I still did not fully acknowledge God's sovereignty as universal and eternal love.

Growing up I was encouraged to pray naturally as if I were talking to a friend or a family member so that what I was saying was genuine and not forced. I remember a boy in my youth group would pull out a chair in front of him when he prayed to remind him that God was present in the conversation. I think these mechanisms and ideologies are well meant, but for me these practices resulted in me treating the Lord like a human.

When we humanize God, we stop dealing with him directly. I am of the firm conviction that the god of my youth was not real. I learned much about the true God, but did not translate that knowledge into devotion to him. I took those ideas and manipulated them into something that made more sense to. In doing so, I stripped him of his universal qualities and muted the immutable in my mind. Though this could seem like a harmless misunderstanding, it had grave ramifications in my relationship with the Lord, especially in understanding how he loves.

Throughout my adolescence, my parents' relationship was strained. My father did not live with us, though he made a great effort to visit us often, but my understanding of family was warped because of this. When I humanized God, I attempted to make him into the father I was missing in my daily life. This was encouraged by friends and youth leaders for obvious reasons. He refers to himself as our Father. The problem for me was that I did not lift my eyes to heaven to see his face and to enter into a relationship with him. Instead, I kept my eyes focused on Earth and attempted to make him fit into the hole in my life and in ways that I could understand. I ignored the qualities of God that are unable to be comprehended by the human mind, and therefore stripped God in my own mind of his true character.

Most of my prayers in middle school and high school were about tests and arguments I'd had with friends. In all of those prayers I was attempting to manipulate the outcome, like a child begging their parents for money or a certain toy. I was listing all of the reasons why I deserved whatever it was I desperately desired. I was not speaking to God as if he is eternal and knows far better than I about the needs of my life. I was speaking to him as if he were a vending machine and as if I could convince him to change his mind of anything.

When I gave God these human qualities, the idol I created was temperamental, like humans. I could not understand the events of my life because the idol I created was not omniscient. The god I imagined felt love for me every day but did not show me love every day, because the way I perceived love was not unconditional, but measured by gifts or praise. When I didn't get what I wanted, I thought that my god was withholding his love.

I was accustomed to living in a society that sees action and performance as worthy of praise, so I lived my life attempting to please the god I thought I knew instead of speaking with and walking with the God I should have known. I spent shamefully little time in prayer during my adolescence. On average, I can estimate that almost all of the spiritual activity of my youth was spent reading and talking about God and rarely to him. But when I did pray, it was mostly asking for things I didn't actually need, or complaining about things I thought weren't fair.

The process of raising support uprooted this issue. When I lost the understanding of the immutability of God's love, I lost my understanding of the gospel's role in my life. I had come to view the good news of Christ's death and resurrection like any other gift I had received. Sure, it held more reverence and was by far the greatest gift I had ever received, but when you receive a gift from friends or family members, that gift is not new every morning. It becomes five days old, ten years old, and eventually falls apart or needs to be replaced. Relying on the Lord each day while raising financial support forced me to recognize the blessings I never deserved, most importantly the blessing of Christ's sacrifice.

I had received salvation when I was a child and placed it on a shelf somewhere in my heart. Occasionally I would dust it off and be reminded of its importance, but it was always an old gift to me, as if it was a family heirloom I had inherited. Coming into the presence of the Lord and treating salvation as an old gift does not work. Christ's blood is newly shed every second of the day since my depravity knows no bounds. When I came to realize that I had already been given salvation that I did not deserve, raising support was something for which I no longer had any expectations. Knowing that I had not deserved my own salvation each second of every day helped me to realize that I also could not deserve any other gift God had to give. Even if he'd already promised it to me, I still did not earn it, and my attitude in prayer should have been nothing but thankful.

I can remember sitting at the dining room table of my mother's house while support raising, staring into my tea cup and trying to logically plot out a strategy. I believe that there is great merit to having systems and organized procedures for raising ministry funds; they foster productivity and momentum. I found, however, that while I was calling and writing to potential supporters, it was highly beneficial to my spiritual growth to have no plan. I spent that morning praying for guidance and confidence. I spent many mornings that summer praying the same prayers and the mornings that I spent in earnest prayer without an expectation or a plan were the mornings that God blessed me most.

Those blessings weren't always financial support. Sometimes they were random phone calls from people I hadn't spoken to in years who greatly encouraged me. Other times they were little gifts of things I needed in the interim between graduation and the mission field. It was the first time in my life where I felt the need to rely on the Lord for anything physical and it was the first time I found delight in relying on the Lord.

I wish I could say that this shift in understanding was permanent and that I never struggled with it thereafter. My year in Bolivia continued to challenge my primitive understanding of the Lord and fortify my new understanding of God's love. A year spent overseas in missionary service, however, is never going to be a year that teaches you just one thing. I had no idea that the year set before me would challenge the very framework on which I had built my life.

3

But let me first

WHEN I ARRIVED IN Bolivia, it wasn't too strange. I had traveled to Panama when I was in high school and Bolivia had similar geographical aspects. I was picked up from the airport at night by a missionary family and I could make out a horizon of palm trees. The road almost felt like cobblestone with so many bumps in it, but it surely wasn't the worst road I'd ever been on. I spent my first night with that family, sharing a bunk bed with a girl who would be one of my students that year. I can remember hearing the intense wind rush across the thin roof, sounding like howler monkeys. Though so many things were familiar, so many things were different enough that I felt farther from home than I'd ever been, and it was the first of many sleepless nights.

The next morning I was driven through the dirt roads of a small section of the city to see the school where I would work. It was three days before the first day of school. Needless to say, I was stressed. I spent the first two days cleaning and organizing my classroom, and then the day before students showed up I buried myself in curriculum, and the book room, trying to figure out what I would begin teaching that week. It was not as easy of a transition as I had thought. I had been overseas before, but not for more than three weeks. The longer I stayed in Bolivia, the more I longed for little things I didn't know I had loved so much back home.

It was difficult to teach in that classroom sometimes, and not just because of physical impediments like losing electricity or a lack of technology. It was difficult to be away from home and get up every morning to teach English. It was also a struggle being my first year of teaching, not yet knowing my own classroom discipline styles and my own organizational preferences. Sometimes it seemed futile and other times it felt like teaching English and literature was the greatest thing a person could ever do. What I came to realize over time was that the days it was hard to teach were the days my heart did not want to be there. I had dreams and desires lingering in my heart that could not come to fruition in Bolivia and those dreams often prevented me from fully enjoying the precious time I had in my ministry.

These unfulfilled desires have been the stumbling blocks of many Christians I know, besides myself. For example, I know many young Christians who have a logical struggle when thinking about the end times. They want Christ to return and see him glorified, but they want it to happen after they are married and have children. I've posed the question back at them "But what about your children? Don't they deserve to get married and have children?"

I typically do not get a response. They sometimes stare off into the distance, as if wondering if there will be a day when no one will have children so that Jesus could come back and everyone would be happy.

In Luke chapter 9, Christ tells three men what kind of sacrifice is necessary to follow him. The first man pledges to follow Christ without even understanding to what he is pledging. The other two men say something a little more interesting. The second man replies, "Lord, let me first go and bury my father" (Luke 9:59 RSV). The third man instigates Christ with, "I will follow you, Lord; but let me first bid farewell to those at my home" (Luke 9:61 RSV).

I don't know how I could openly call myself a devoted follower of Christ when I had stipulations so similar to theirs in my own heart. When God put Bolivia on my heart and told me to go, I had so many "but let me first" arguments. I knew the calling was for so much more than just teaching English. I knew that the Lord was not asking me to take another short term trip.

But even in the mission field these thoughts grew rampant. I felt the call to stay for a longer term, but I could not rationalize staying when I had a fiancé at home waiting for me. So many prayers were saying "Yes I'll return, but after I get married and only until I have my first child, then I'm coming home to America." It took months to be able to say "Yes—on your terms, however you want them."

Teachers feel this power struggle often with their students. I have had so many high school students attempt to make my classroom run on their terms. Students often try to bargain their way into getting what they want. They want to sleep through today's lesson and promise to stay awake for tomorrow's, or they want to turn their homework in three days late and still get full credit because they tried. They want to have the lesson outside, or have the last five minutes of class to relax. It is not uncommon. I would be rich if I had a penny for every time a student asked "could you push the test back to Tuesday?"

Perhaps they thought that life was better the way they had it planned. Perhaps they really did believe that they could learn better if they had another day to study, even though they knew they would choose to do something else with the extra time. What I came to realize fairly quickly was that when they were held accountable to deadlines and rules, their behavior improved. They learned and earned excellent grades. When they insisted on their own terms and did what they wanted and how they wanted it, they learned very little.

It seems so trivial, does it not? The difference between taking a quiz on a Tuesday instead of a Monday is so small. Both are toward the beginning of the week and both would take equal time out of my lesson plans. But I'll tell you the difference—one requires discipline while the other does not. One requires that you are within the parameters of the class preset by the teacher, abiding simply because they asked you to. The other requires no responsibility because you negotiate the rules to fit your convenience.

Why would God ever allow us to know him and choose our own rules created from our depravity? Whom would that honestly benefit? Surely it would not benefit the Lord because from our own depravity we cannot have true fellowship with him. And surely it would not benefit us because our unwilling heart would prevent us from listening to his will.

In that first year of teaching, I quickly learned that when a student had a bad attitude about an activity, their bad attitude spread like a disease to the people around them. Suddenly instead of just one student not wanting to comply, I had six. So I found that if a student did not want to participate, it simply took a brief speech that went a little something like this:

"You have a choice to make. You can choose to participate in this activity, or you can choose to sit outside, but I will not allow you to get in the way of the success of someone else. If you choose to fail this assignment by not participating, that is your choice."

And, to my surprise, I had students who willingly chose failure. The first few times I did it that year, I felt like a horrible teacher because my students failed. I thought that I was the worst teacher in the world and that they were failing because of me. But the more I had these conversations, the more the students chose to participate and ultimately succeed.

Life on their terms led to failure, and I had to let them realize this. I could not force them to take part in my terms. Forcing them led to rebellion and the falling out of multiple students. I could not do that to my classroom. Success in the classroom is dependent on authentic participation.

After they chose failure multiple times, students noticed their grades in my class deteriorating. I often got the question: "Why am I failing your class?" The ones who had learned their lesson would ask it in a worried way and then talk with me about how to improve. The ones who had not, would ask me why I gave them an F on certain assignments. I would look straight into their eyes and tell them: "That was the assignment that you chose to not complete." If this conversation was happening at the end of the semester, they would hurriedly say that they promise to complete it as they reached their hands quickly to the bottom of their backpack, knowing exactly where the paper was.

I love my students. I cried many times over the ones who chose failure that first year of teaching. Some did not— some failed initially because they struggled in my subject and those students worked hard and were able to pass my class in the end because they put in so much effort all year long. It was the students who willingly chose failure that broke my heart.

There is an uncountable amount of times I can recall in my life where I posed these same arguments with the Lord. Any circumstance that was unpleasing or uncomfortable for me was something to blame him for and a reason to not do as he had asked of me. At the end of the first semester of the school in Bolivia, I was beginning to face some of those deeper rooted contentions and I found that it was finally time for the Lord to break them.

Though we were dating at the time, my husband flew down to Bolivia to visit me during his winter break from college, just after I had finalized the grades for my first semester of classes. A few weeks later, he proposed and we had many talks about our future, and specifically our future in missions. They were serious, because we knew the consequences of choosing a missionary life. We knew the hurt our family could feel especially if we chose to have our children overseas. We knew the pain we would experience to be estranged from our friends.

These were some of my stipulations preventing me from following the "classroom expectations" of the Lord. Scriptures clearly state that we are to "Go therefore and make disciples of all nations . . . " (Matt 28:19 RSV). I wanted that calling to be pushed back just like my students wanted quizzes and essay deadlines to be suspended. I had desires I wanted to fulfill first.

While struggling with these life decisions, I learned that I can't blame God for my own selfishness. It's funny how we call it bitterness or a "loss of faith" when we let something separate us from him. In my life, it's most often blatant selfishness and I've tried so many times to blame him for it. I have made the declaration that he called me to missions and therefore it is his fault that the desires of my heart to raise a family in America or have a successful American career might not come to fruition.

I have tried so many times to make my stipulations, to say "Yes, I'll follow you, but let me first. . ." and that "let me first" comes in so many shapes and sizes. I have publicly declared that I will follow Christ, and yet I willingly choose to ignore his calling. I bargain for more security, more time, and more luxury despite the fact that time and time again he says that's not his way. This cycle always results in my complaint of not being able to "feel" God's love. In my mind he has withdrawn his love from me because he will not give me the desires of my heart as I believe he has promised me (Ps 37:4 RSV). But the scriptures clearly state to "Take delight in the Lord, and he will give you the desires of your heart. Commit your way to the Lord; trust in him, and he will act" (Psalm 37:4–5 RSV). The more time I spent seeking the Lord while in Bolivia, the more time I found myself seeking the desire of his heart instead of chasing the dreams of my own.

4

The greatest impediment

Transitioning to life in South America was not an easy feat. Any missionary can tell you a long list of things that are different or difficult to bear in their country of service. In Santa Cruz de la Sierra, Bolivia, for instance, you do not flush toilet paper. Taxi drivers need to be given directions to many places you want to go, so you must know how to get there before you hail a cab. Their main public transit system is "micros" which are very small buses obviously meant for people shorter than six feet tall, and in some cases shorter than five and a half feet. Stores are not a standardized commodity; the commercial industry is primarily made up of markets and those markets are open air and tightly stuffed with both goods and people. Most roads are unpaved, and many that are paved lack lines to indicate how many lanes of traffic there ought to be. Electricity can turn off at any point for any reason. Wi-Fi becomes unavailable during times of intense wind. Ants bite you, always. Electric showers will shock you if you touch them and will sometimes shock you even if you don't touch them.

The list could go for miles.

The point is not that Bolivia is wrong. The point is that it is different from the culture I grew up in. Likewise, to a Bolivian, America is quite different. Developmentally, we formulate a cultural understanding of ourselves and our society as we grow up. Some of this understanding is taught to us, though most of it is contrived non-verbally. We watch others be praised or shamed for various actions and we accumulate a list of unwritten rules that govern how we operate.

When you move to a foreign country, those rules must change. File them away for when you return to your home country and start a new list for the time being. I found when I arrived in Bolivia that if I attempted to impose my list of unwritten American standards, I stood out or was uncomfortably ostracized from my environment. Bolivia was not meant to conform to me; I was meant to conform to Bolivia.

I can remember one of the first weeks I was in the country a few of us first-year single missionary women were driven downtown to start the application process for permanent visas. On the way there, our truck was hit by a horse. I repeat myself: the horse hit us. After being rammed into by a wild stallion, having the back passenger window of a missionary's car shattered and our nerves equally rattled, we eventually made our journey downtown a few days later.

My assumption was that we would arrive at some state department building, most likely with large white stairs in front and perhaps with a statue or two lining the stair case and big columns in front of the doors. Obviously, I expect-ed government related buildings to look like buildings I was accustomed to see in Washington, DC. I was absolutely surprised when we pulled into a dirt parking lot next to what appeared to be a house. Our missionary guide ushered us in one at a time to fill out a form and have our picture taken on a standard point-and-shoot camera by a woman in immaculate heels and tight red jeans.

At a later date, we had to go downtown to a specific lawyer to have another paper notarized. When you walk through the bustling center of the city, the Spanish word for lawyer, *abogado*, is everywhere. We were looking for a lawyer with a specific number next to his title. I can remember counting at least nine lawyer offices all with numbers very close to the one we needed. I felt practically exhausted by the time we found ours.

After taking pictures and hunting down our lawyer, we made our way to a government building. When we were given passes to enter into the building, we sat outside of an office with all of its blinds closed. We went into that office one at a time to speak with a person, in Spanish, about our intention in staying in the country. This person was dressed in either police or military apparel; I could not tell the difference at that time. Had I known better, I might have handled this situation with ease. Under the circumstances and my lack of understanding of my surroundings, I felt like I was being interrogated and that my life was on the line.

When all of that was over with, the process was still not done. I had been allowed into the country on a temporary visa but needed to apply for residency. This required us driving out of the center of the city to another residential area that looked like duplexes to me. We stood in a line outside of one white duplex that looked identical to all the ones around it, but somehow everyone knew this was the house to complete residency applications. We waited and received numbers to eventually have our application looked over and approved. Even after all of these steps, my ID card was received by my field leaders in June after I had already left the mission field.

This example is obviously trivial in nature, but it proves the point that a transition to a foreign country involves the loss of the familiar and the embracing of the new. If you expect people to interact with you like an American would, you will be very confused and sometimes offended by their behavior. If you expect systems and processes to be conducted in the same manner as your home country, you will be frustrated. When I stopped expected and started observing, I learned how to appreciate the Bolivian culture and assimilate to it.

I stopped trying to shake hands with everyone and learned to lightly touch the shoulders of women I was greeting and to kiss them on the cheek. I also learned not be frightened when random women kissed me on both cheeks and introduced me to all of their children. I quickly realized that if I introduced myself to market vendors and visited them often, remembering their names and asking about their family, they would give me fairer prices. I also found that if I needed to get somewhere and back, I could hire the same taxi driver and get a lesser fare than I would paying for two one-way trips. I began to allot more time for things because I'd discovered that a couple of errands that would take an hour in America are full-day expeditions that require a lot of walking through hot sand and a significant amount of dehydration.

After a few short months in Bolivia, I found that I had shed my American "self." I felt Bolivian and I equally felt so estranged from my American family and friends that it was as if I had known them in a previous life. I even came to resent aspects of American culture as I appreciated the Bolivian culture more. What was difficult about this assimilation was that even though I felt Bolivian, I was not received as a Bolivian, for obvious reasons. It was as if I truly belonged to a third culture that was neither Bolivian nor American.

I was attending a church that was somewhat near my house. If you were to look at it on a map, the walk might appear to be a nice morning stroll. Since there was no bus that could take me from my house to my church, I had to walk through the heat and the sand, only crossing one paved road to get there. Bolivian heat is different from American heat. It feels like the sun is sitting directly on your shoulder, injecting every inch of your body with its scorching rays. Thus, a distance that might have taken twenty minutes to walk in America took me forty minutes one-way, passing through multiple neighborhoods, mangy dogs, and whistling men to get to a small church building with open windows and two electric fans at the front of the meeting room.

While the walk renewed my tan every week, it also drained me of all energy before I even got to church, and soaked my clothes with sweat. My water bottle was empty by the time I arrived, and trying to engage in Spanish at that point was quite difficult seeing as I could barely think profoundly in English. The young adults would break off from the main service and have a Sunday school in an adjourning brick room with small windows near the roof that offered little relief from the heat.

This Sunday school was run by an older man who was missing a few teeth but made up for it with his passion for the scriptures. He was not a perfect teacher, however. I often felt on Sunday mornings that it was my duty to correct him, not out of arrogance because I was not able to teach that Sunday school better than he, but out of love because I saw room for the gospel in his messages where the gospel was previously missing. Whether or not I corrected him, and whether or not I said anything, that man spoke with so much passion that I often wondered if I would ever have as much passion in my faith as he had in his.

Over time, however, church began to feel like a job. It wasn't that the people at the church had put me in a position of compromise, or had asked me to do anything past my capacity. It was simply that I did not feel like I was growing at all in my church. It took so much physical energy to simply arrive, and so much mental capacity to function in Spanish, that I rarely had the ability to hold deep theological discussions in that Sunday school room. Adding on the fact that the discussion in my young adult's group often required correcting, I sometimes felt very little joy when returning to my home in the early afternoon, wiped of all energy or desire to do anything else.

I questioned at one point if I should find a different church that could better support my spiritual needs. I felt that God was asking me to stay, not so that it continued to feel like a job, but because he wanted me to shed my old spiritual culture as I had so willingly shed my American culture. I could not approach that church with an unteachable spirit, as if I had nothing to learn and was only there to help. That's not the purpose of a community. I also could not attend that church with just the intention of seeing my own spiritual growth. I had been in ministries where both of these were my goals. When I focused on correcting others, it was always out of pride and never out of love. When I focused on just my own growth it was selfish and I rarely felt like I had true community with anyone.

I knew the Lord was asking me to surrender my old habits of seeing ministry as a place just to teach or just to learn, but I failed miserably at it. I became my own greatest impediment. As I updated my blog regularly, I found that my American identity wanted to write about grandiose things that would impress my friends back home. I wanted people who financially supported me to know that their money was going to good use and that I was not wasting time. I let my pride and my goals get in the way of God's goals.

Like many struggles that year, this was a cycle. There were times when I was ardent in my prayers to assimilate to God's spiritual culture and his strength and his love were my source of life. There were equal amounts of time where I was securely devoted to my own purposes and my own pride steered the wheel of my actions. It was in these times that I felt exhausted, bitter, and fruitless.

One example of this was morning devotions. I was supposed to conduct a short devotion with my first period class each morning. Some mornings we didn't, honestly. Some mornings I forgot or I felt like I didn't have enough time. Those were the mornings I was focused on my own success and running on my own fuel. There were even mornings when I did lead devotions on my own fuel, and it was mostly just retelling lessons God had taught me in my own life that I thought would be helpful for my students.

My intention in those lessons was honest, but that specific application is like a substitute teacher teaching whatever they think that class of students needs to know instead of following what their teacher has planned for them. The mornings that I sought the Lord for his wisdom and his desires for those students, I was inspired to teach things I would have never planned. We had discussions that moved hearts and those discussions built me up in my own faith as well.

One morning, I felt strongly that our devotion should discuss the parts of the body of Christ. I could remember years of Sunday school and youth group studies on this part of the first letter to the Corinthians and the importance of all the parts within the body of Christ. I could recite this verse from memory: "If the whole body were an eye, where would be the sense of hearing? If the whole body were an ear, where would be the sense of smell?" (1 Cor 12:17 RSV).

In our brief discussion, a student asked if someone could be two body parts. I responded that the body parts were symbolic of particular roles in a Christian community, not that a singular person was actually a hand or just a foot. This put the question to rest, but the idea of being multiple body parts stuck with me.

It was December at this time, and I had been teaching in Bolivia for five months. I had battled bronchitis for two weeks, and would have two more weeks of it to come. I was attempting to teach four different grade levels of secondary English, shepherd my first period students in their theology during devotions, and somewhere inside of me was the equal desire to bring all students to Christ or into closer relationship with him. I was coaching the JV girls' soccer team, trying to disciple girls at the school, attempting to be involved in the youth group or support the youth group with deep relationships with all of my students, attending a church with the intention of helping it in some way, and trying to be a helpful and supportive roommate to three other single missionary women. Needless to say, I was exhausted.

I spoke with a good friend about it later that afternoon and through tears I had to admit to myself that I am not the entire body of Christ. I was still carrying my American culture with me in my spiritual walk and in my new surroundings. Growing up I had played multiple sports, multiple instruments, participated in multiple musical groups, multiple school clubs and activities, and still attempted to have an excellent GPA with a perfect social life. I was groomed to be a Jack of all trades and I let myself believe that this was the norm. I even let myself transfer this notion into my spiritual life.

No one expected me to do everything. The missionary field is unique in that there is always more work than workers. It does not matter how many people you send to a foreign country, their mission will expand and they will branch out to more places and more people. No one can take all of that responsibility on their shoulders to ease the load of everyone else. An attempt to do so is equal to self-harm. Likewise, thinking that you can be the entire body of Christ is foolish and prideful. It is not a coincidence that Christ himself traveled with close companions while completing his ministry.

A few weeks into my winter break one of my roommate's and I stumbled upon an online quiz that asked us to list all of the books of the Bible in order. We were sure, as missionaries, that we would ace this test without blinking. We missed one: Haggai. Upon failing the quiz, and subsequently feeling like awful Christians, we decided to read it since neither of us had ever opened the book of Haggai. Little did I know that a tidal wave of spiritual reproach was heading my way.

When we arrived at verse nine, both of us let out a deep sigh as if we had been stung with a spiritual prod: "You have looked for much, and, lo, it came to little; and when you brought it home, I blew it away. Why? says the Lord of hosts. Because of my house that lies in ruins, while you busy yourselves each with his own house" (Hag 1:9 RSV).

There are certainly many obstacles that stand in the way of a missionary. There are cultural impediments and spiritual battles. There are financial struggles and a constant abundance of work to be done. But time and time again I found that my greatest struggle was with my own inadequacy and my own pride. I was constantly doing what the Lord warned Haggai against—building up my own house, or proving my value through works, before building up the house of the Lord.

I made the mistake of comparing myself to other missionaries and wondering how teaching English in a classroom was achieving the same amount of spiritual "greatness" as teaching scripture to those who have never heard it. I would look at the work of other missionaries and say: "I'm not doing enough." This is a lie rooted in pride and insecurity that must be staved off with the same intensity one would evict a robber from their home.

Scripture tells us to "Be sober, be watchful. Your adversary the devil prowls around like a roaring lion, seeking someone to devour" (1 Pet 5:8 RSV). This lie of insufficiency came each time to steal my motivation and my energy. It was from the devil and I did not often enough set up defenses against it. I would let it slowly seep in, unnoticed, and I would begin to agree with it until "I'm not doing enough" became an unspoken mantra. I would foolishly do this again and again as if I had not learned the last time. Unfortunately, the "I'm not doing enough" morphed each time into different expectations. First it was not doing enough at the school, but the next time it was not doing enough with my church, or with outreach, or with helping other missionaries, or with fostering community amongst young missionaries, or any other possible job I could think imagine.

I had spent most of my college years building up my knowledge about the Lord and not cultivating my relationship with the Lord. The college environment creates a general attitude of learning and I approached my faith with that attitude. It was a great time of intellectual growth and I do not regret the amount of knowledge I gained, but I do regret the lack of time I put into the application of that knowledge.

When I first met with the executive director of my mission on my way down to Bolivia, this was one of his greatest concerns for me. I had spent three years being discipled and pruned for spiritual leadership, but all within the context of intense communal fellowship that held me accountable to my spiritual disciplines and showed me what to do next. I had not spent any time outside of that framework building my disciplines on my own.

I did not see the danger in this. I had heard from many people of the importance of personal spiritual discipline, but within the campus environment, I did not see the imminent need. I never had a reason to hold myself accountable when everyone else was asking me about my personal studies of the scriptures. The weekly meetings were a time of teaching led by ministry staff members and though I helped lead the meetings, I had nothing to do with the instruction. I attended those meetings to learn.

The mission field was a drastic change from that environment. Though people are always interested in the spiritual development and practices of others, it's not their job to check in with first-year missionaries on their personal spiritual disciplines. Even if it were part of their job, it would not be their top priority on the mission field. Additionally, I had three years to develop the deep community on my campus with very few worries or strains on my life. In Bolivia, I had three days of culture shock before my ministry began and no time to cultivate deep relationships with fellow missionaries to hold me accountable to my personal conduct or my ministry conduct before diving into my work.

My own lack of spiritual discipline prevented me from having deep fellowship with the Lord and with other missionaries. I was not accustomed to studying the scriptures entirely on my own. Sure, I'd spent many hours poring over passages on my own during college, but always with the knowledge that someone would ask about them or would want to help me understand them more. And I'd read through many exegetical and Christian texts, but most of those books were read through a Bible study or with another friend at the same time to discuss it. I had hardly spent any time picking up books just for me because I wanted it for myself.

I quickly found that this was not going to work on the mission field. The accountability and fellowship was not a college ministry. It was an international ministry and just like the culture of Bolivia was drastically different from the culture of the United States, the culture of fellowship on the mission field is naturally different from that of a college Christian organization. My first steps in self-discipline were futile until I discovered that I could not live life by myself. I could not travel in the city on my own. I did not have enough physical strength to help me survive a Spanish speaking world without a mental breakdown or to survive the oppressive heat without passing out every afternoon for a three hour nap. I needed God more than I'd ever known and it took being stripped of my spiritual structure to realize it. I needed discipline in my walk with God that would complement my spiritual community, not a community that would create discipline for me.

5

Let there be darkness

THE "PIT" IS A name I coined for the location or time of suffering in my life. When I come to the pit I do not despair long, for the Lord my God is with me, guiding me through the hottest fires so that I may be purified in his name. The pit is not a place of useless torment or a period of desolate life. It is simply a time when faith must be made strong.

I heard a saying halfway through my one-year service that seemed quite trite and almost childish, not to my surprise considering that it was shared by a teenager. But, the phrase grew to become a staple in my life in the months to follow: "When you are going through something hard and wonder where God is, remember—the teacher is always quiet during a test."

It is possible, and most probable, that this resounded with me because I was a teacher in a classroom experiencing this on a regular basis. A student would get confused on an assignment that they needed to complete individually and instead of asking me to reword a question or give them some guidance, they would simply ask: "What's the answer to question eleven?" and I would always reply with a smile, "I can't tell you that."

When a student has been trained to function with certain skills, has been given a whole group opportunity to observe those skills from the teacher, and a small group or partner experience to try them out and see their peers use those skills, it is essential that each student then completes the task on their own. For if they cannot accomplish the task without any help or instruction, they have not truly learned the skill.

Likewise, if I were to swoop in every time a child raised their hand and simply give them the answer they were looking for—would I have taught them anything at all? If all they ever knew was how to write down what I say, how would they ever be able to write or think for themselves?

There were multiple low points in my one-year abroad where I could not feel the presence of the Lord. It felt as if he had left me. When in reality, I am now quite glad that he did not respond to my anxious pleas, my temper tantrums, and my shenanigans, simply because I was forced to do what he had very well taught me to do. I had two options while in the pit: I could do what I had been trained to do, or I could give up my mission entirely.

And might I note: giving up your mission when you are 4,000 miles away from home in a developing country, and no plane ticket until another five months has passed, is not an option.

Each time I reached the pit it did not take me long to realize that God had placed me there with a purpose. Whether I felt estranged from my family, inadequate as a missionary, lost as a Christian, or utterly abandoned by anyone I ever knew—each time I looked for answers in the wrong place. I would search high and low for a reason and a rationale to explain my situation and comfort my despair and in all of those searches never did I once turn to Christ first.

I could create a tremendous list of the sufferings I experienced while in Bolivia. Many of these sufferings seem trivial now, but when added together they were a mountain of pressures. I experienced continual physical trials from illnesses to injuries. I experienced relational issues and classroom discipline issues. I experienced the loss of two great things, one more trivial than the other: my engagement ring and the death of my future father-in-law. With each suffering, I felt lost. Sometimes it took weeks and sometimes it only took moments for me to acknowledge the hand of God in my life at these moments.

I found my way to him eventually, and every time I found myself rereading the book of Hosea. In chapter 2, the Lord says of Hosea's wife: "Therefore I will hedge up her way with thorns; and I will build a wall against her, so that she cannot find her paths. She shall pursue her lovers, but not overtake them; and she shall seek them, but shall not find them. Then she shall say, 'I will go and return to my first husband, for it was better for me then than now'" (Hos 2:6–7 RSV).

When I sit in the pit and I feel the walls closing in on me tightly, it is my natural instinct to cry out to God for a reason why these injustices are happening. When I watched my friendships wane and my relations with my family become distant and cold, I sat in the pit asking why the Lord had neglected me. When I labored grievously day after day on my own strength trying to prove something or earn respect, but ending each day with more emotional pain and less energy than the day before, I would beg the Lord to simply fix everything. When the fabric of my heart felt like it was tearing in two from the emotional grief of being separated from my fiancé, I would pray the Lord would allow us to speak on the phone because I felt alone in a freezing pit of despair with no one to save me.

But he was there. He was withholding the emails and the phone calls, setting a temporary embargo on them. He was hedging up my heart piece by piece as I desperately grabbed at anything I could find until nothing was left. He knew it would hurt, but even more, he knew what would be gained from it. To enter the pit meant to be forced to lean solely on Christ and find all of my value, joy, and strength in him.

To give one example, though there are many to choose from, I was robbed only a few weeks before the end of my year in Bolivia. I had been with two other single missionary women in broad day light on a normally busy street. The street that day was oddly empty and we each were carrying large purses full of valuable things. I lost books that were close to my heart. I lost an expensive camera given to me as a Christmas gift from my husband's family. I lost all of the cash I had with me.

At the same time, my computer died a horrid death and I could not use it to call home to anyone. My bank card, which was not taken in the robbery, had been voided by my bank and a new card was reissued to my mother in Pennsylvania. There was not enough time for her to mail it down to me before I came home, but I still owed rent, and needed money for groceries and transportation, as well as a mandatory exit tax at the airport.

I literally had nothing. I was hedged in with no means of moving anywhere. I had to rely on others for transportation and funds. Though it's comical now, I was not laughing then. I was bitter.

I was bitter for so many other things than these circumstances. I had been bitter for quite some time. A few months prior to this experience was when my husband's father had passed away. My husband and I were engaged at the time and the idea of his father not attending our upcoming wedding was heart wrenching. He had become a source of hope and restoration in my own heart and his absence was a source of extreme resentment in my heart towards the Lord. This was not the only struggle in my heart, but it was most certainly one of the most potent.

I had spent the last months in my classroom with barely enough energy to teach, let alone be an ambassador of Christ to my students. And now that I had finished my time in my classroom and was slowly packing up my life in Bolivia, the Lord hedged me in. He refused to let me leave the mission field on these circumstances. If I had not been forced to focus on him and to set right these circumstances in my heart, I would have taken my bitterness with me on my return home and I can only imagine the hideous divisions in my heart that would have occurred thereafter.

While in this specific pit, hedged up with nowhere to go, I surrendered my bitterness to the Lord openly. I explained in complete honesty the points of contention in my heart and the deep hurt I was struggling with. I did not run from him and I did not withhold my pains so as to nurse them into deeper quandaries. I openly prayed for a change of heart and refocusing of my vision. I did not desire to continue in despair and spiritual treachery. I could have flipped to every verse listed on the bookmarks in my Bible that offer general hope and prosperity. I could have reread the passages that typically lift my spirits, but the Lord had something else to teach me.

The opening chapter of the book of Psalms left me feeling like a foolish idiot. That opening chapter, though it's only six verses long, clearly articulates everything I need to know in how to be content with the plans of the Lord. After reading it, I figured that I might as well memorize it as a means of prevent this despair at any other point in my life:

> "Blessed is the man who walks not in the counsel of the wicked, nor stands in the way of the sinners, nor sits in the seat of scoffers; but his delight is in the law of the Lord, and on his law he meditates day and night. He is like a tree planted by streams of water, that yields its fruit in its season, and its leaf does not wither. In all that he does, he prospers. The wicked are not so, but are like chaff the wind drives away. Therefore the wicked will not stand in the judgment, nor the sinners in the congregation of the righteous; for the Lord knows the way of the righteous, but the way of the wicked will perish" (Ps 1:1–6 RSV).

Could it be more easily spelled out? I have heard frequent jokes from Christians that they have wanted God to send them messages in the mail, or in a text, or even a note attached to a brick thrown through their front window because they were just so desperate to understand how to find happiness. But in reality, the answer is waiting for them at the beginning of the Psalms. Blessed is the man whose "delight is in the law of the Lord, and on his law he meditates day and night" (Ps 1:2 RSV). I can outright tell you this much—the times when I meditated on his law day and night God never hedged me up in a pit.

6

The assault

WHEN I WAS FOURTEEN, I took my first venture out into the mission field. I signed up, hastily, to go for two weeks into the jungle of Panama, eager to do something daring and have cool stories to tell my friends. I did not yet realize that when you sign up for missions, God takes you seriously.

I found myself having a hard time dealing with the realities of the jungle and life outside of the States. I also could not reconcile how God could love the village people as much as he loves me if I am blessed with luxuries and they are not. I asked one of my leaders that evening about it and we had a wonderful talk about God's providence and plan for each person.

In the middle of his explanation, I interjected "but if God has a wonderful plan for each person, why do bad things happen to believers?" He smiled at me and gave me an image I will never forget. Using his hands, he formed a battlefield and drew a line with another finger to show where the front lines of both armies were standing. He then asked me a simple question: "If a line of enemy soldiers is attacking you, who do you shoot? Do you shoot the soldiers in the front or the people hiding in the woods?"

I had never been introduced to the idea of spiritual warfare before this point and was hardly even aware of the spiritual realm, but over the years as I experienced more supernatural events and became alarmingly aware of the enemy's grip on my culture, I saw his point. If Satan has waged war on mankind—he's going to take down the people openly engaged in the fight. And if I openly engage in battle by being a missionary on the front lines, I must be prepared for war.

Are demonic encounters a guaranteed experience on the mission field? No. But I would say it is foolish to expect a missionary term to be free of struggle and spiritual warfare. It is also foolish to apply a humanist view point to any phenomena. When I rationalized the events of the spiritual realm, I ignored the hand of God in my life.

Why do I mention these things? Because the goal of the devil is not to simply distract you, though distraction and deviation are common struggles for Christians. I was living in a country where I could not be distracted, except by my own self-made busy life. When I quieted that lifestyle and sought the Lord for strength and fellowship, there was nothing to distract me. I was living in a desert region with nothing exciting to draw my gaze away from the Lord.

I remember having a conversation toward the end of my year in Bolivia with my husband, who was my fiancé at the time. We were on a phone call discussing and we ended up discussing why miracles and demons are not as prevalent in the United States as they are overseas. We had lots of reasons and our conversation went down many paths, but the ultimate conclusion was that while miracles and demonic activity certainly exist in the United States, the average person needs not encounter them to lose their faith. The culture alone supports a mentality that will dismantle the Christian mindset.

I noticed in my time in Bolivia that there was a plethora of single female missionaries and only one single male missionary. I've heard that this is a current trend. I do not judge the men of the world for this ratio, but it does make me wonder. If my roles had been reversed, if I was still in college and my husband was the one who felt called to go overseas before we were engaged, would he go? I do not doubt his reverence to the calling of the Lord, or his desire to follow the Lord's will. I do, however, understand the cultural expectation in America that would have pressured him to stay and be a "bread-winner" saving up money for us to be married with great financial security.

I don't know what that pressure feels like, but I do know how the cultural pressures of America affect the Christian heart. The desire for success, financial security, admiration, and community are strong. Though they could come from the Lord for his goodness, they have been construed so as to build up the individual. The importance of individuality and self-reliance is rampant and I cannot ignore how this plagued my heart.

The cultural pressures are much more than self-reliance. To see the looks on the faces of family members when discussing whether or not my husband and I would consider having our children overseas is enough to make my heart rip at its ends. Would we surrender our desire to return to the mission field so that we could be assured to have our children where it would make everyone happy? Absolutely not. Does our unwavering devotion to the Lord's call for our life make that decision emotionally easy? Not at all. The notion of settling down has taunted me my entire life. Growing up in a military family and having to say goodbye to every best friend I'd ever made in my youth was painful. Not having a single house to claim as a home for more than a handful of years at a time was not enjoyable, and the American dream of settling in a home and starting a family of my own in a permanent place is something that I still battle today. This culture of self-reliance, family, success, and security is not easily shed.

Whether or not this culture was formed and cultivated by the devil, it was a horrible decision to allow it to enter my heart and take hold of me. My adolescence was wrought with angst and confusion. My relationship with the Lord lacked authenticity until I went overseas where I was stripped of that culture and forced to be completely naked before the Lord. I had nothing to brag about. I had no trophies or accomplishments to make me feel better about my own depravity. It was during this ripping of self-important culture and earnest searching for God's culture of humility and grace that I found spiritual warfare to be most evident in my life. I do not find that to be any coincidence.

I was most surprised by how easily the feeling of isolation or helplessness caused physical weakness. The scriptures clearly point to the necessity of a community in Christian faith, but I never realized how this community was integral to the physical functioning of a person. All it would take in any moment was the slightest feelings of loneliness, and my entire productivity and happiness could unravel in an instant. I could have the most wonderful day in my classroom and arrive at my house to find no one home, when suddenly a feeling of abandonment would sweep over me. After months of battling this, I learned to pray against it, but for many months it was as if the very breath was taken out of me for no reason at all.

Even working with people from different places and different mindsets can be a challenge. That challenge is natural, but the flames of that challenge can easily be fanned by Satan. When you have missionaries from different mission organizations, ages, educational backgrounds, and specialties it makes the workplace of a school exciting and diverse. I had so many opportunities to learn from people I never would have met in America. Likewise, the devil had so many opportunities to pit us against each other. As a first-year teacher, first-year missionary, and first-year post-college graduate, I felt like I had a lot to prove, especially to myself. All it took was criticism in a harsh tone, and I was a puddle of tears. Did I accept constructive criticism throughout the year? I begged for it, but I was not always in the mindset with a willing heart to receive it.

Spiritual warfare has a lot of baggage with its name. I encountered supernatural enemies that provided me with the scariest experiences of my life. Looking back, however, I can clearly see that those encounters were not my biggest obstacles. My biggest obstacles were when my weaknesses were being used to prevent my productivity. I was undone when my own pride or insecurity was being pressed upon. All it took was a small jab to leave me down for the count. A supernatural experience would lead me straight to prayer because I always respond to fear with prayer. I have not, however, always had the spiritual discipline to pray in response to pain. I have spent many years responding to pain and suffering by looking for comfort or toughing it out. It is of no coincidence, then, that the devil's battle for my ministry was through pain and suffering, not supernatural phenomena.

When our engagement ring went missing, my husband and I didn't really know how to handle it. I never got the chance to see the ring because it went missing before he proposed to me. It was in his pocket one minute, and gone the next. Whether or not it was taken by some supernatural force, or it simply fell out, the main contention in my heart for months to come was that God did not prevent it from happening. I had to rationalize again and again in prayer and in thought that God had a greater plan and a purpose for this experience. The God who loved me and had poured out blessings upon me and spared me from so much of the horrors in this world would not have allowed this to happen without a specific purpose.

I will openly admit that this specific purpose I was searching for did not come. I was looking for a marvelous, miraculous reason for my ring to have gone missing. I was looking for such a grandiose reason because deep in my heart I honestly believed that ring was stolen from me. I saw the engagement ring with all of its American cultural implications. It was not just metal and rock; it was love, romance, and self-worth. Its absence was a constant source of emotional dejection despite my conscious ability to admit that it had no eternal significance.

It was difficult to answer the questions from friends about its disappearance. Every question, every glance, and every reaction was painful to receive. They were painful because they reminded me of all of the hope I had placed in a material object I thought I had deserved. While I never got my big miraculous reason for its disappearance, I did have the assurance that this experience consistently reminded me of how much the things of this world do not matter. I knew that if my husband and I were to enter a life in ministry, there would be greater sacrifices to come and this loss would seem trivial to what might lie ahead.

The second half of my year in Bolivia was a struggle for this very reason. I had trials, which had wounded me, that were easy targets for emotional defeat. Every day was a new chance to have an old wound reopened. Between the ring, the passing of my father-in-law, the easy pain of loneliness, the basic struggles of my first year of teaching, and the trials of living in a developing country, any day was an opportunity for tears. With each chance of pain came a chance for dependency on the Lord. When I was leaving America, my greatest hope for the mission field was that my heart would be humbled and reformed with greater dependency on the Lord. I found that no matter the trials that came, no matter the pains in ministry or my personal life, each offered their own chance to learn again how to depend on the Lord for strength, hope, peace, and joy.

When I was done teaching for the school year and preparing to leave Bolivia, I was petrified that the dependency I had learned to have with the Lord would fade when returning to America. I could make lists of things I knew would distract me from my walk with Christ. The lack of having my own car, television, and stable internet was enough to provide me with at least an hour of reading and prayer in the morning, if not another hour or two before bed. I had become dependent on the disciplines I had learned while in the mission field and I feared that my old lifestyle which lacked spiritual discipline would sprout its roots and grow again upon my return.

7

The greatest weapon

BEFORE TRAVELLING TO BOLIVIA, I would sing hymns and worship songs in church and shed a few tears when a line of the song would refer to heaven. I desired heaven ravenously because I desired to be close with the Lord and to see his face. Looking back, I think part of that desire sprung from insecurity in my own faith. I wanted to know that he was real.

When returning from Bolivia, I sang those same songs and cried for different reasons. I had seen his power and known his voice on Earth. The power of his existence in my life on Earth was so overwhelming that to imagine his infinite glory in heaven brought me to tear-filled awe.

I had been on the mission field for eight months when I was physically afflicted with dengue fever. I had been through all kinds of trials and experienced all kinds of physical strain, but it was nothing compared to this. I woke up one Saturday morning with signs of dengue fever; the most evident was the beginnings of the rash on my back. I writhed in my bed from the excruciating pain shooting through my bones. I described it as metal rods being shoved through the middle of my bones as if to shatter them from the inside.

I can remember the sleepless night full of rank sweat and no respite from the oppressive heat pouring in through my window. Another missionary had let us borrow her oscillating fan and it was a miracle beside my bed. I had the strangest dreams and experienced hallucinations that I swore were real. I had no doubt that my death was imminent. I was so dehydrated within my first night that I felt my throat had begun to shred itself into two pieces.

People prayed, though. If everything I have said so far has not yet emphasized the power and necessity of prayer, let me make it evidently clear at this moment: prayer is the strongest weapon you have against the devil and against your own flesh. I had posted on my blog about my dengue symptoms and people back home sent me emails letting me know they were praying. While I writhed through the night, just before dawn, approximately 24 hours after the symptoms had started, they subsided.

Is that abnormal? Absolutely. The pain and fever alone typically last one to two weeks. The full recovery of strength and mobility takes several weeks. I was walking freely within two days. No rash, no pain, minimal stiffness. Sure, I shuffled around like a grandma for a day or so, but within no time I was a Spring chicken.

I could fill pages listing the amount of times God healed me and spared me pain while I was on the mission field. From a thousand little headaches that I eventually learned to pray about instead of seeking medicinal help to the serious illnesses and calamity, God was faithful to restore my health and protect my body.

Within a month of being in Bolivia, I had an oven explode in my face. The gas had been leaking into the oven chamber and I went to bake some bread. After lighting the ignition, there was a loud explosion resulting in burns on my arms and my face. Within twenty minutes of asking friends at home to pray for me, my burns disappeared before my eyes.

I had a broken toe that was healed in one day. I had the pain of a thrown out back completely removed. I had flu symptoms absolved from my body. I had burning ant bites disappear and a lost voice reappear. In the name of Jesus, I saw the calamities of this world in their true form: passing and powerless.

More importantly, the power of continual prayer and big prayers was equally astounding. After a terrible encounter with dogs, I prayed that the Lord would spare me from ever being attacked by a dog again. For the remainder of my time in Bolivia and the two years I've been in America since my return, I have not had a single dog even bark at me.

While returning to America, I was praying about what to do next. One morning while waking up, I heard a distinct whisper say to "teach in Alexandria." I shook it off as the remnants of a dream initially, but I began to pray about it. I applied to over twenty-six schools in the greater northern Virginia region, and at the beginning of the next school year I was offered a teaching job in a school in Alexandria, VA.

I understand why I did not pray fervently when I was a teenager, or even my first years of college. I had a humanized idea of God and did not fully understand who he was or what his desires were for my life. I was not actively engaged with him and did not seek his face for strength, redemption, or hope. The mission field broke this from me and my prayer life became something I'd always desired: a conversation with the living God. It is a conversation I did not know I desperately needed and a conversation I can no longer live without.

I never realized before just how much a lack of prayer apathetically affected my spiritual life. It's as if not speaking with the Lord directly correlated to a disbelief in his existence. When my faith was based on sight or proof and I did not pray, it was a self-created failure. I was not asking for anything in faith, and in seeing nothing lost any faith I'd had previously. I was completely ignorant to the life that could be found in prayer and just how much I was missing by ignoring this spiritual discipline.

The mission field taught me many things, mostly of my own deficiency and desperate need for God's provision. I found the truth of what it meant to be a child of God and to find my cultural identity in his character. But, if I learned nothing else from my time on the mission field, I learned that penitent and continual prayer is both life saving and life giving.

8

The scars of a mission

I WOULD BE A liar if I said coming home was easy. Boarding the plane felt like treason in the depths of my heart and landing in the States felt like a strange amalgamation of nostalgia and vertigo. The mission field opens your heart to so many problems you never knew you had and so many problems you never knew the world has. Handling that knowledge can be a very painful experience.

One of my greatest mistakes in all of my times overseas was to personalize ownership of my ministry. After two separate short term trips to Panama and one short term trip to Sierra Leone, I would have thought I'd learned how to distance myself from ownership, but I obviously didn't. I found myself at the end of my time in Bolivia still fighting the belief that these students were my responsibility and that if I left no one would take care of them.

There was no guarantee of anyone coming down after me to replace my teaching position or lead the youth group at the school. There were large gaps created in this particular mission field and my heart was wrought with worry. I felt guilty for going home, even though it is clearly what the Lord was asking of me. I did not yet fully understand that those children were his and not mine, and that he loves them far greater than I ever could.

In addition to that, there was the typical culture shock adjusting to the United States. I cried the first time I went into Target. The abundance of luxury was so overwhelming that I wanted to hyperventilate and hide in a clothing rack. It did not matter what I needed to buy, everything was frightfully expensive because I was converting all of the dollar amounts into Bolivian currency and comparing how much it would have cost in Bolivia. Everything seemed like an enormous waste of money and what used to be a pleasurable place to live suddenly seemed volatile.

I wanted to get rid of everything I owned. I was packing up my old things from my mother's house to move them down to Virginia and I felt like none of it belonged to me. It all belonged to someone I used to know but who had been missing for many months. She wasn't coming back and she certainly didn't want her things.

She didn't know her friends, either. Meeting up with people I hadn't seen in 11 months was strange. Not only had we been apart, but I was a different person than when I had left. My heart was burdened, heavy, and beaten. Some people who I'd even kept in contact with felt like complete strangers to me the first I saw them again.

The hardest pill to swallow transitionally was the regret. I would reread some of my blog posts or think back on how certain events passed, regretting my own foolishness or selfishness. The lessons of humility and servanthood that I had to learn the hard way and that adversely affected some of the people around me were tangible scars on my heart. I would replay conversations in my head as if somehow I could change their outcomes.

I had a heavy heart for many months because I was not satisfied with the work I had done. I knew based on the times I had spent in earnest prayer that my time in Bolivia could have been more fruitful and more Christ-centered. I knew that his works in Bolivia could have been greater if I had listened more.

It took me the entire summer after I returned to come to terms with the fact that his plan supersedes my regret. Whether or not I could have done things differently, the way that my time was conducted and the hard lessons that I had to learn were a part of his perfect plan and to argue that they should have been any different is heretical.

My greatest fear in returning to America was that I would lose the unadulterated faith and relationship I had gained with God while I was in Bolivia. I was afraid of the noise and distraction old habits in the States would bring back into my life. One fortunate circumstance of serving a longer term in missions is that it creates new habits that defy old ones. It felt weird to continue these habits of penitential and continual prayer in my old circumstances and surroundings, but the desire and the necessity for these habits did not fade.

Did I continue to weep? I still do. If I spend enough time thinking of my students or their families, I cry uncontrollably. My heart has been captured for a people and I pray that the fervent love I carry for them will never fade no matter my calling in life. Though there are painful scars that I carried away from my mission field, the joys of fellowship and love that I gained greatly outweigh any trials.

Nothing taught me more about diligence, spiritual discipline, and perseverance than my time on the mission field. It was the only place in the world where the only option for survival was to practice the beliefs I had professed for years but upon which I rarely acted. It is my hope that if the Lord has called you to serve in overseas missions, you would not hesitate. To go is to give up that which you should already have surrendered, and the loss of it will be the greatest addition to your faith.

www.ingramcontent.com/pod-product-compliance
Lightning Source LLC
LaVergne TN
LVHW051711080426
835511LV00017B/2855